THE JOURNEY OF

"EMBRACE"

Anne Marie Powers

Anne Powers is a Fine Arts major at the
School of the Art Institute of Chicago. She
grew up in the South suburbs of Chicago, in quaint
part of Orland Park. She works mainly in Oil Paint
and Ceramics. Anne is scheduled to graduate with
her BFA from the Art Institute in spring of 2015.
She traveled to Tanzania and Kenya, Africa in 2012
on a Therapeutic Art trip through
Global Alliance Africa. Anne is greatly
interested in working with special needs and the
process of therapy through art. This series of
paintings, "Embrace" is done
through the inspiration of the children she worked
with while in Africa. Anne was touched by there
welcoming and loving embraces, closeness even
with a language barrier, energy and spirit. Currently
she is attending school and will continue
this series of expressing emotions and spirituality
through portraiture.
Annemariesart.com

Global Alliance For Africa

"Global Alliance for Africa transforms the
lives of orphans and vulnerable children
affected by the AIDS pandemic in sub-Saharan
Africa by partnering with grassroots
organizations
to design and implement innovative
economic development programs that enable
families and communities to become
self-sufficient Our focus on economic
opportunity ensures a brighter future
for the poorest and most vulnerable in
Africa and provides a solution to the
cycle of poverty.
We promote:
*Empowerment & Self-Reliance
*Sustainability
*Accountability
*Innovation Solutions"

www.globalallianceafrica.org

"Our Notion about Happiness entraps us.
Our idea of happiness can prevent us
from actually being happy.
We fail to see the opportunity for joy that
is right in front of us when we are caught
in belief that happiness should take a
particular form."

-Thich Nhat Hanh.

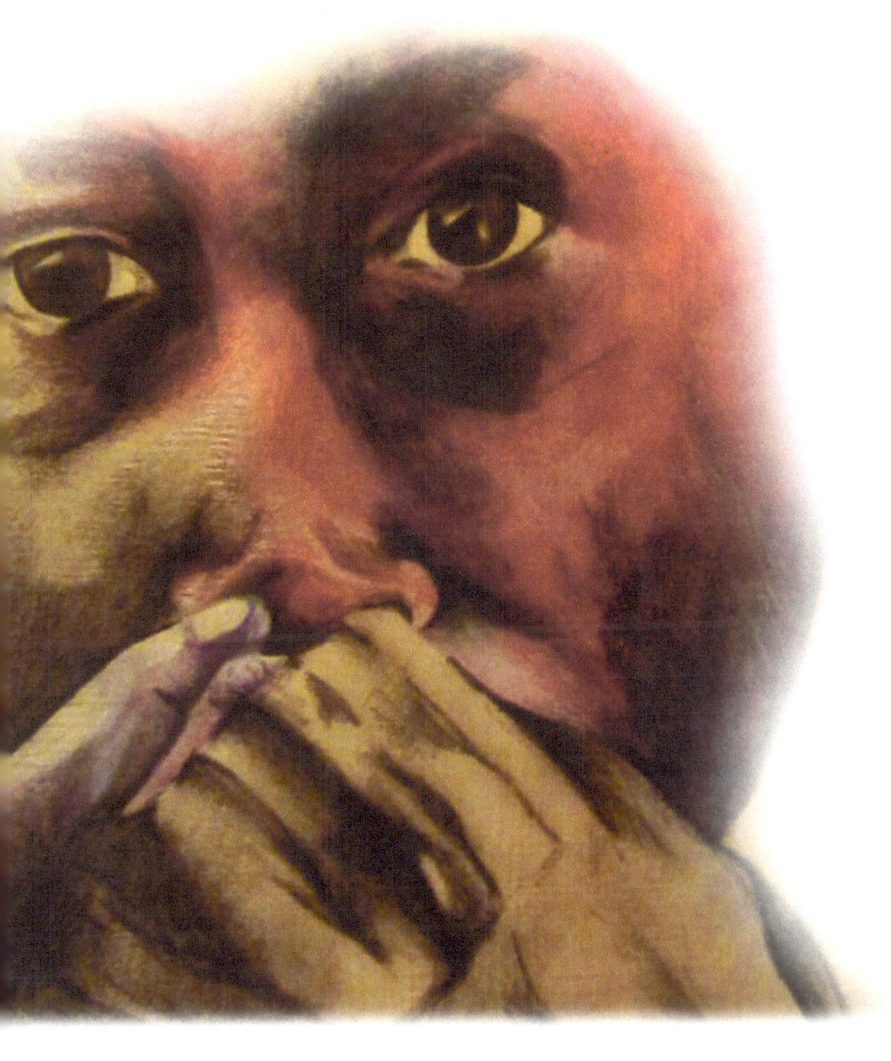

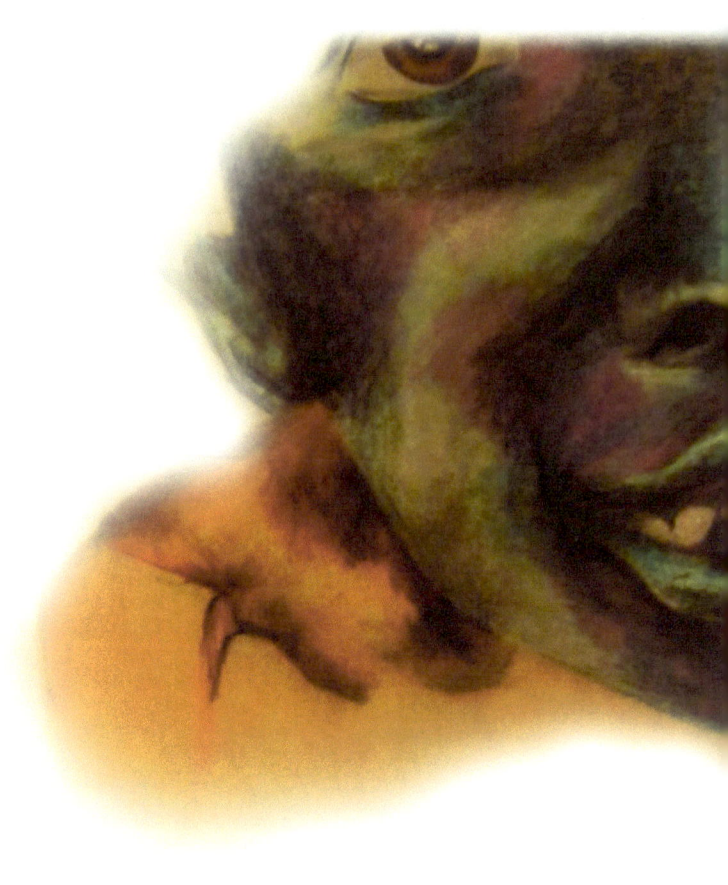

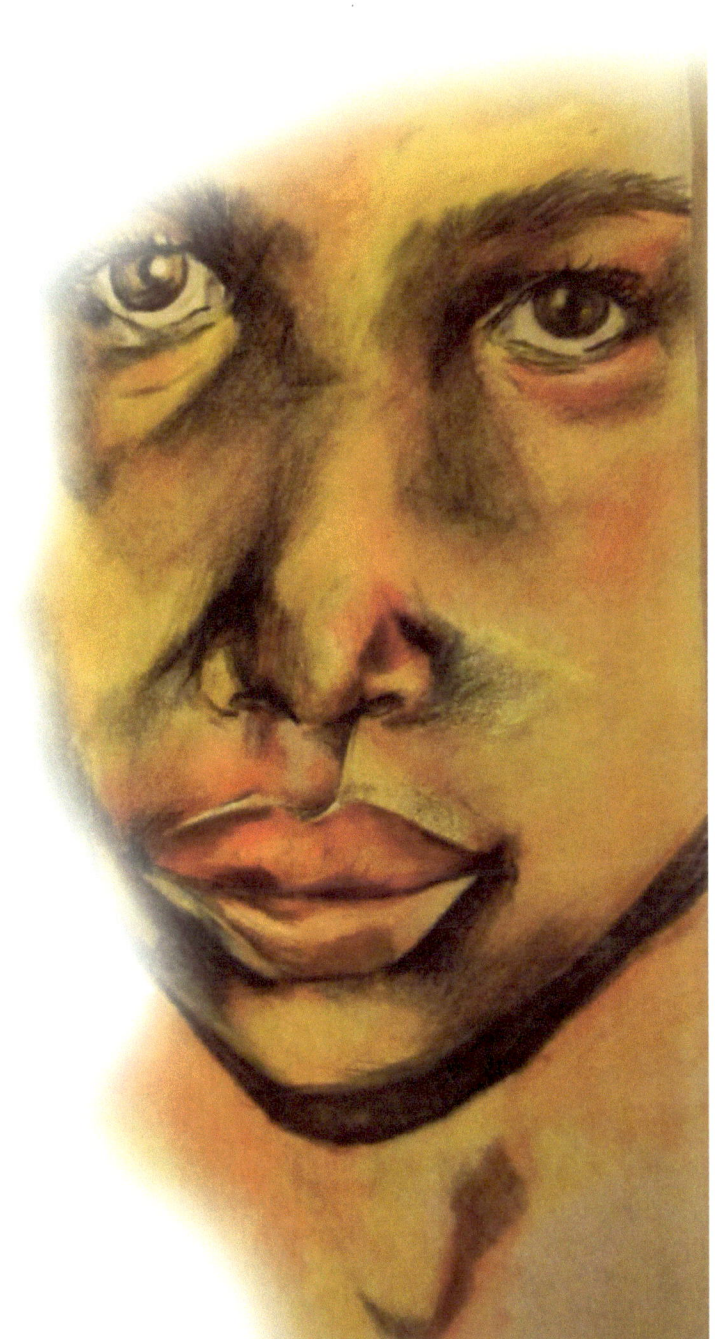

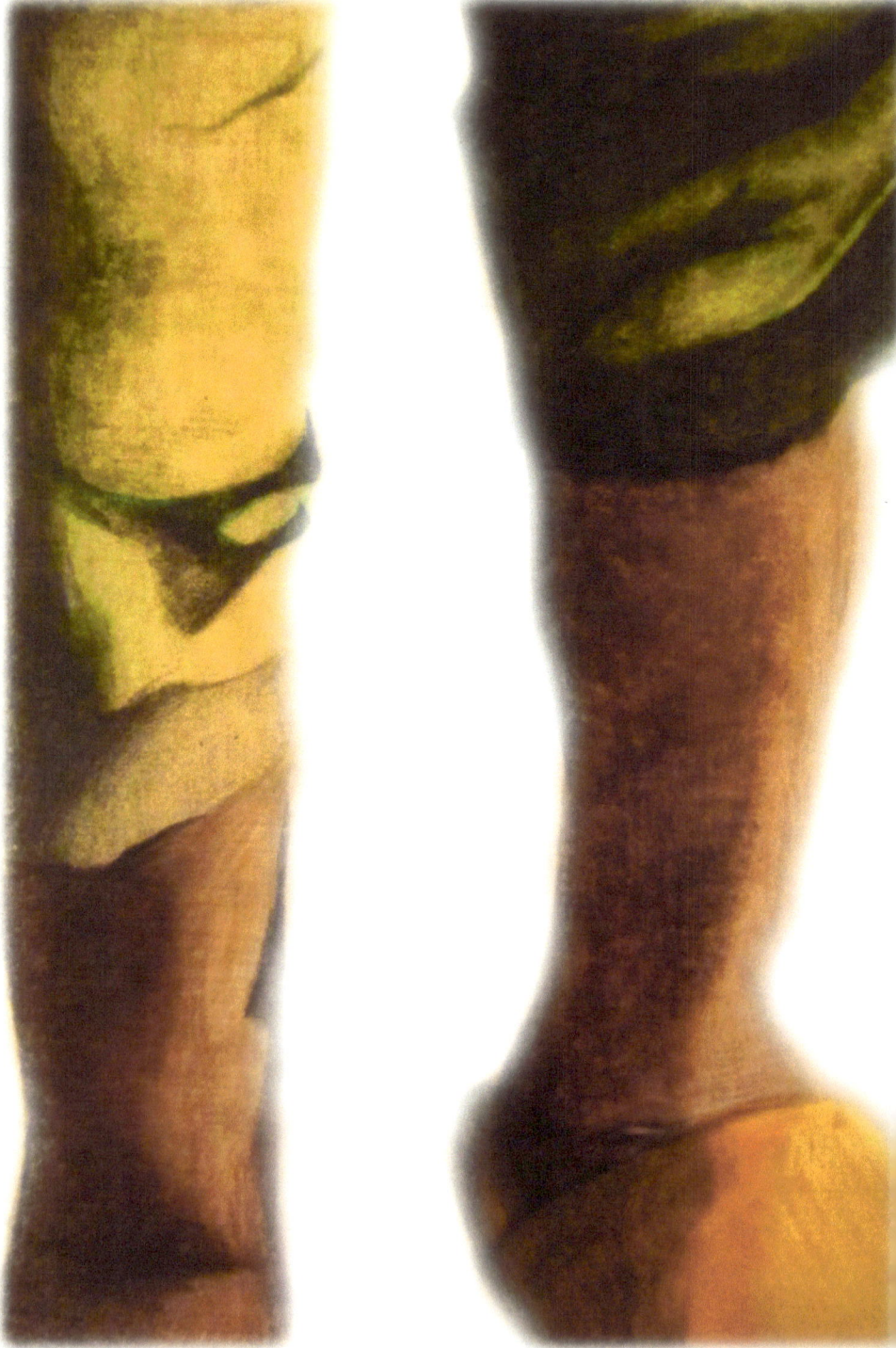

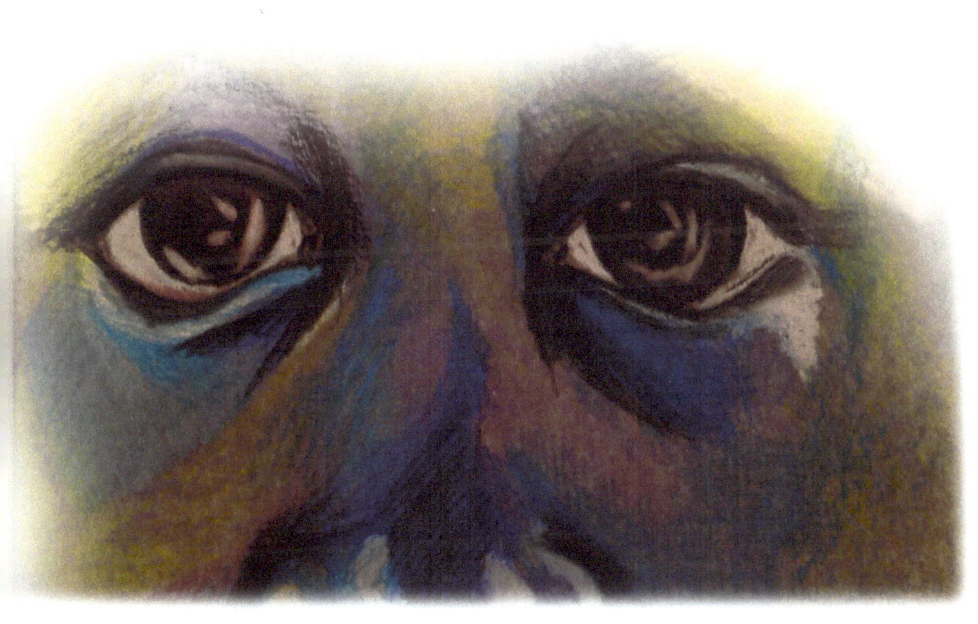

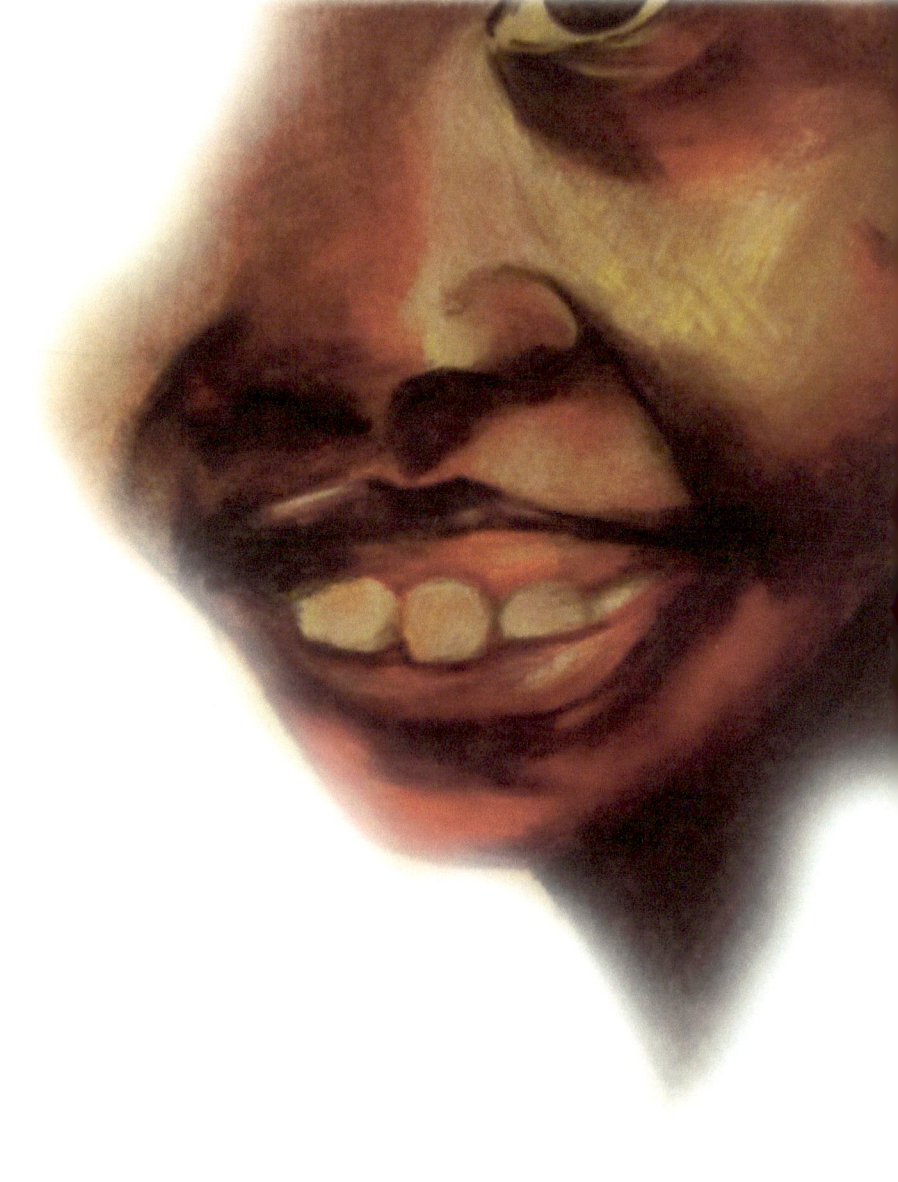

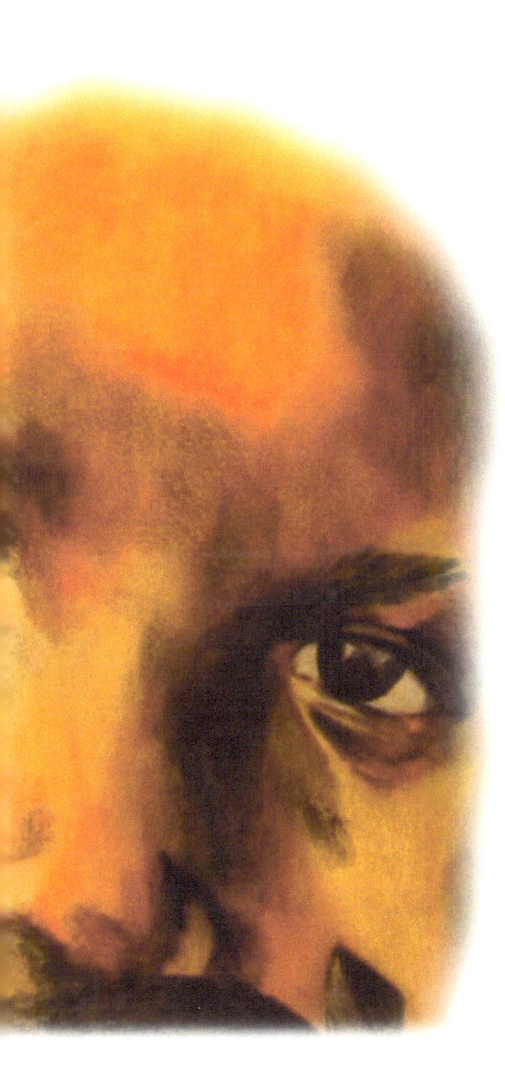

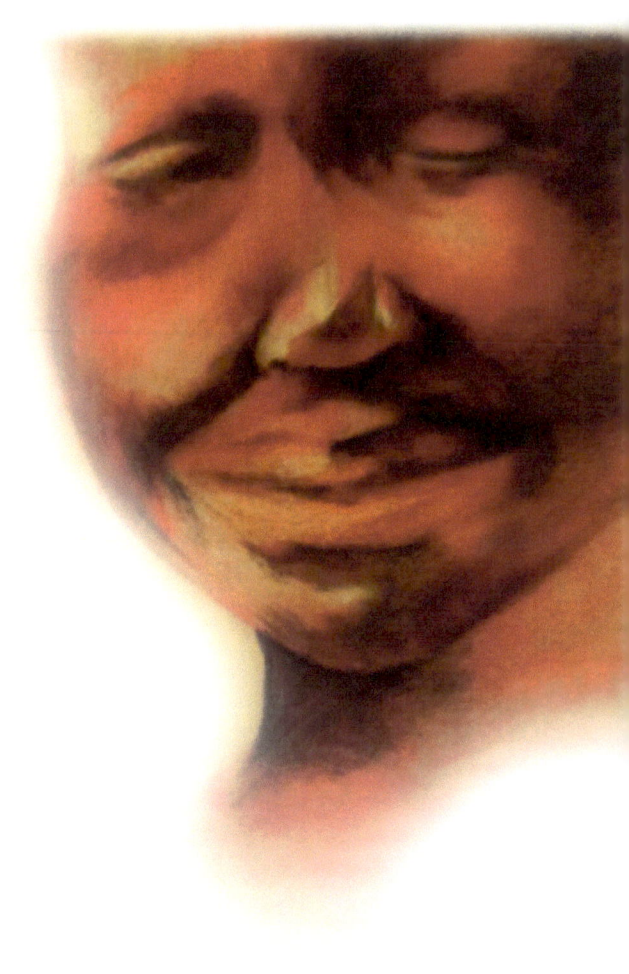

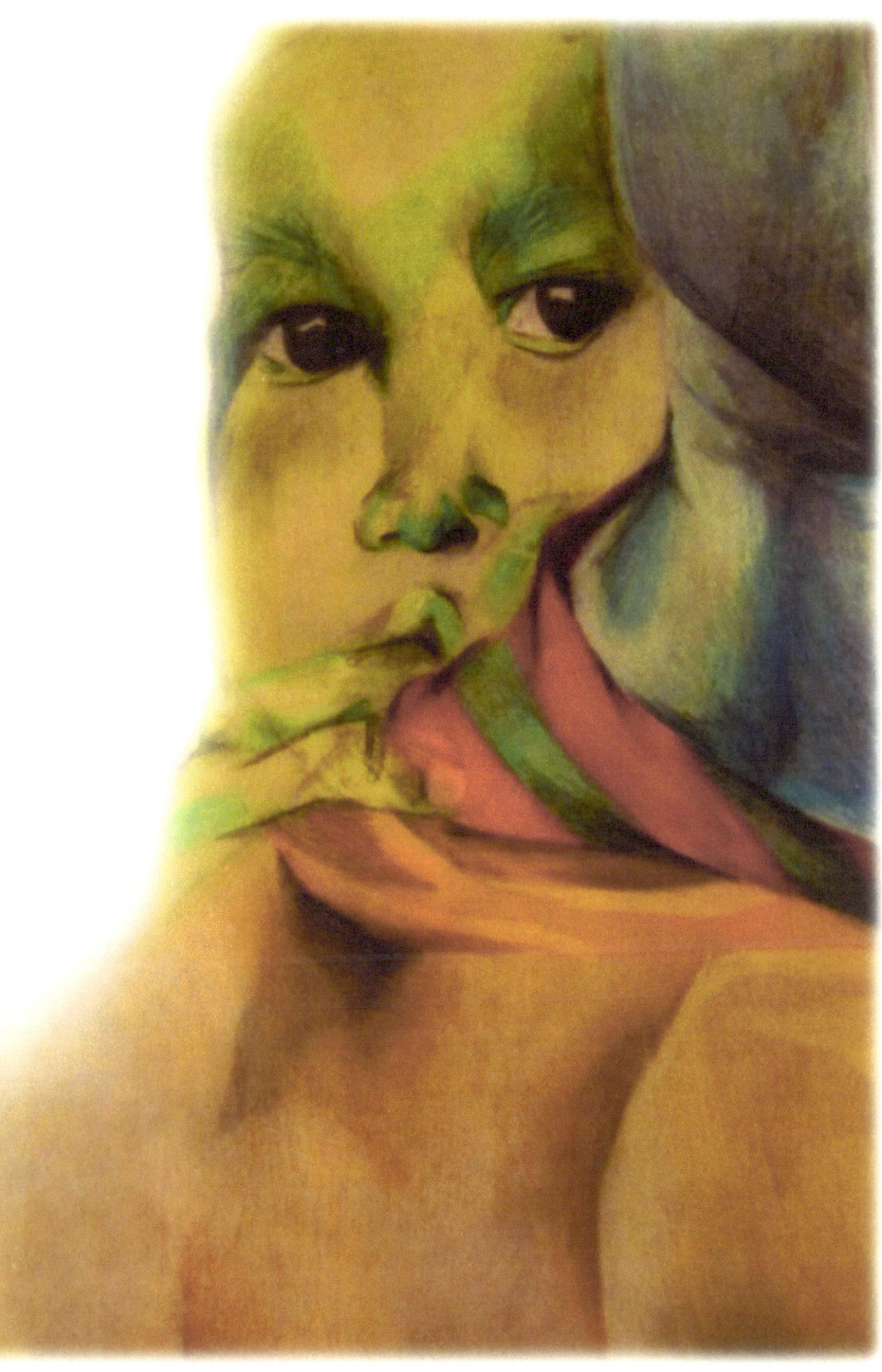

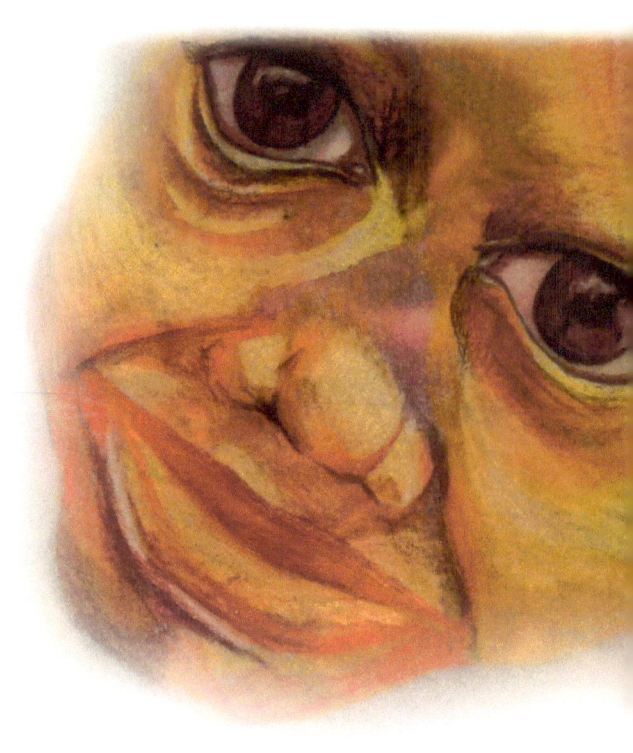

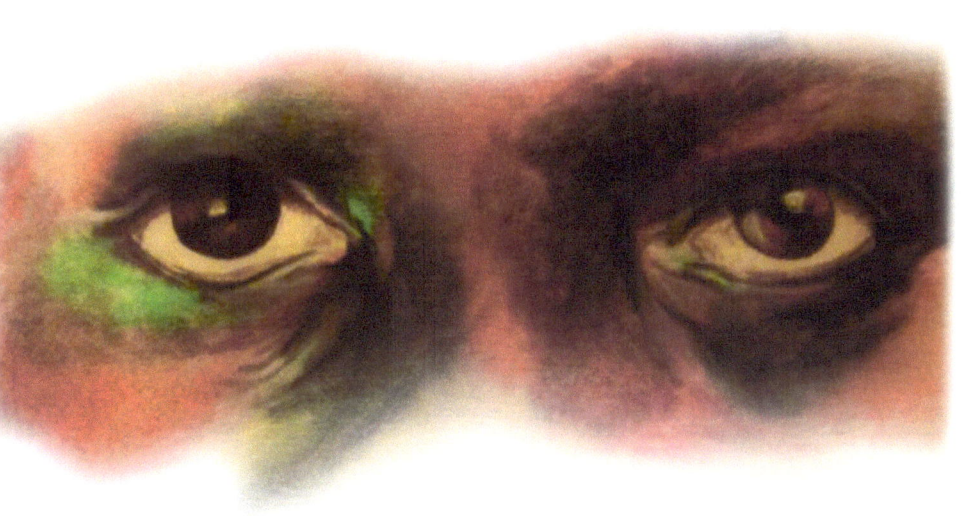

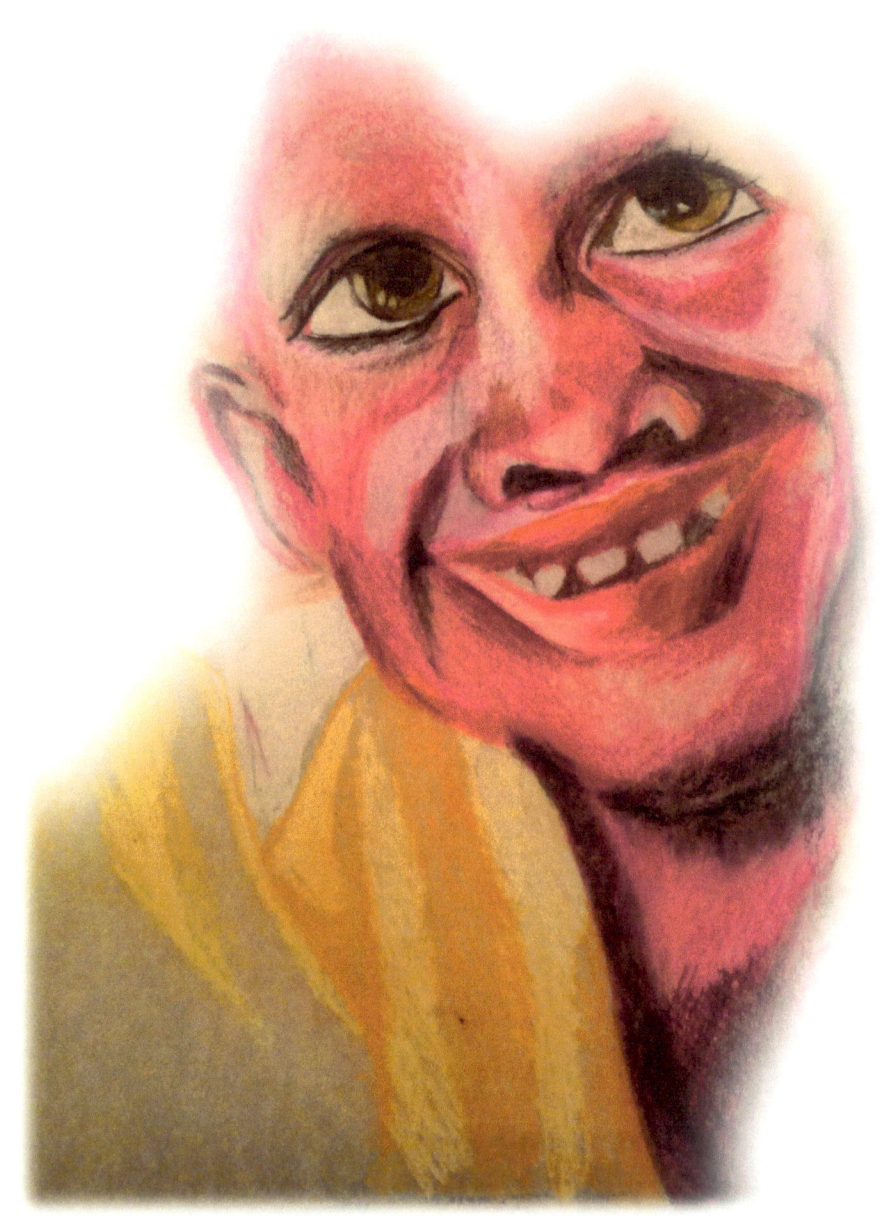

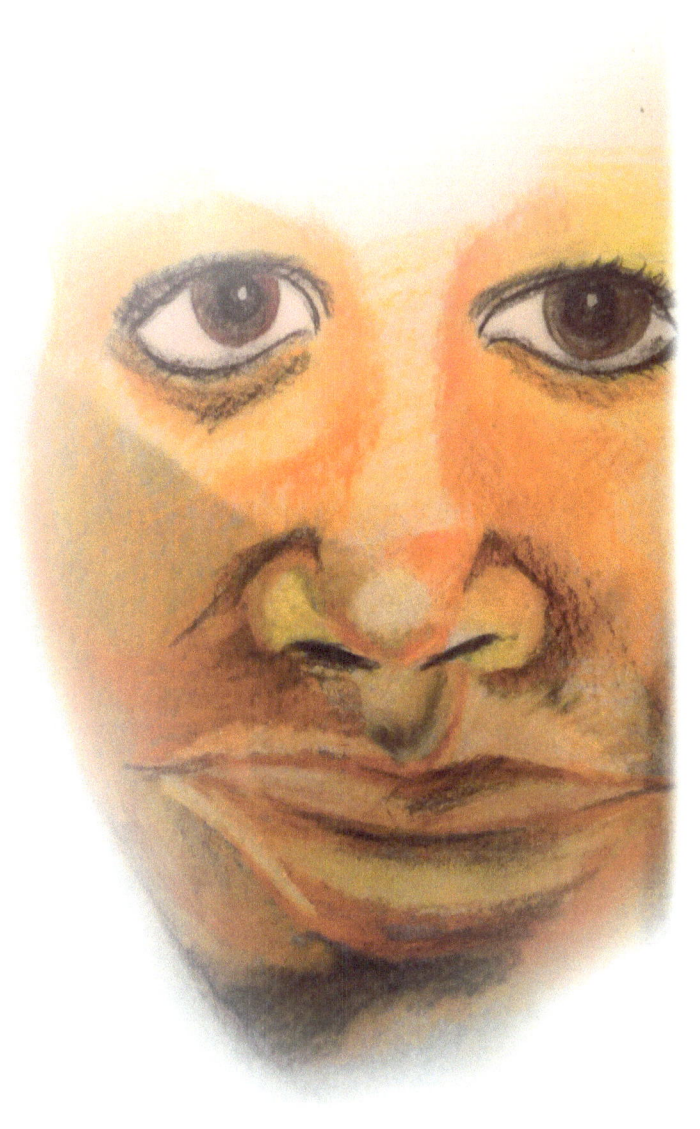

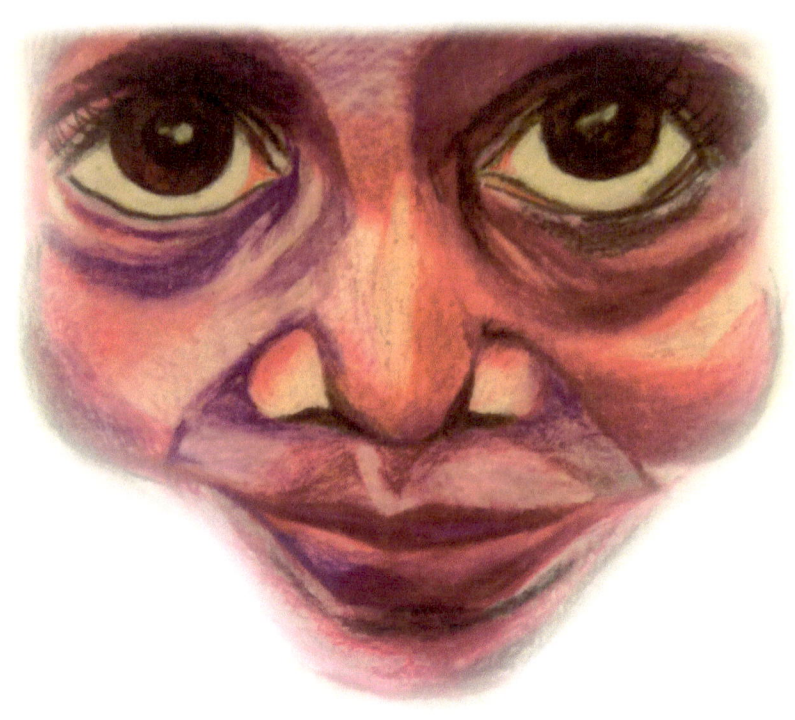

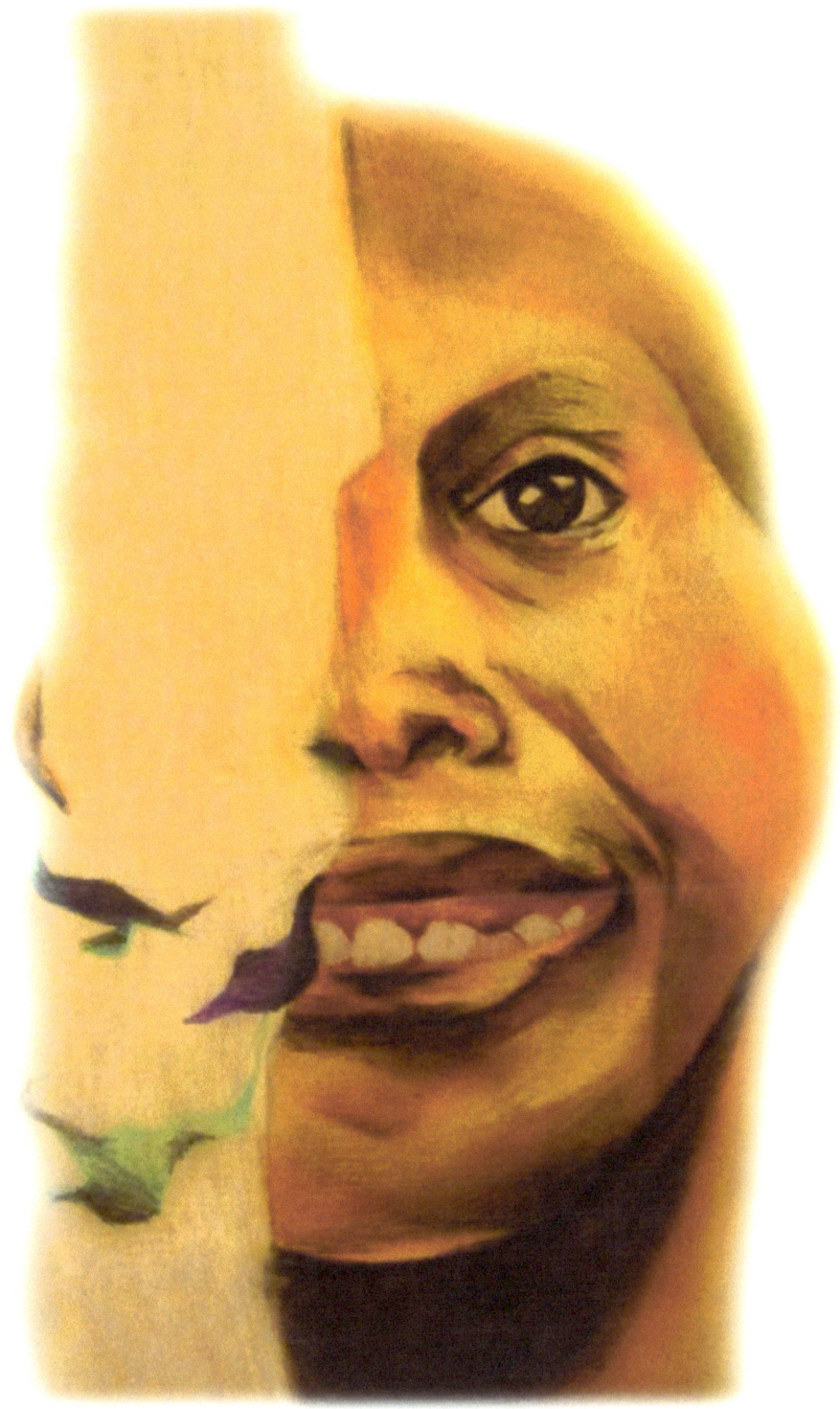

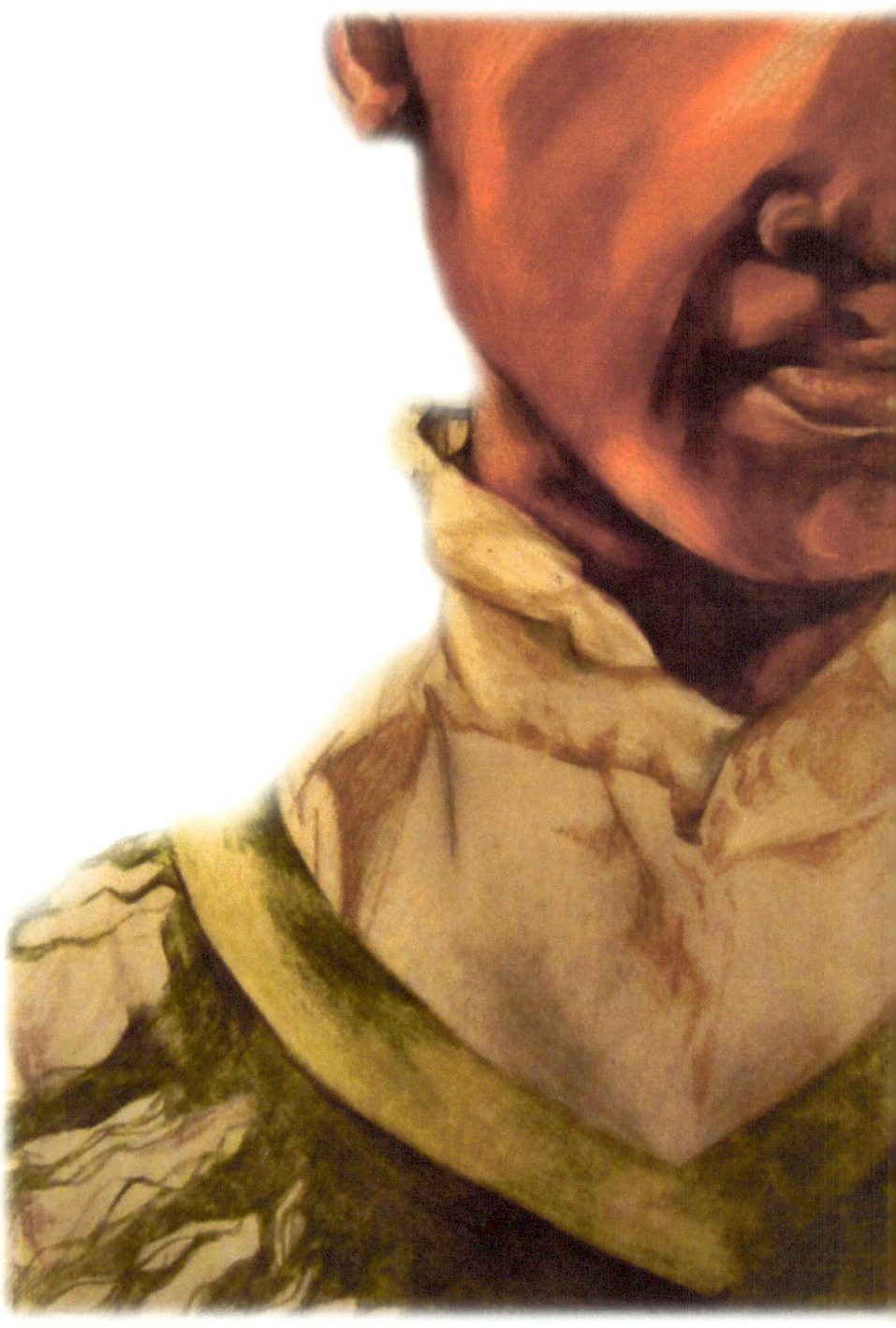

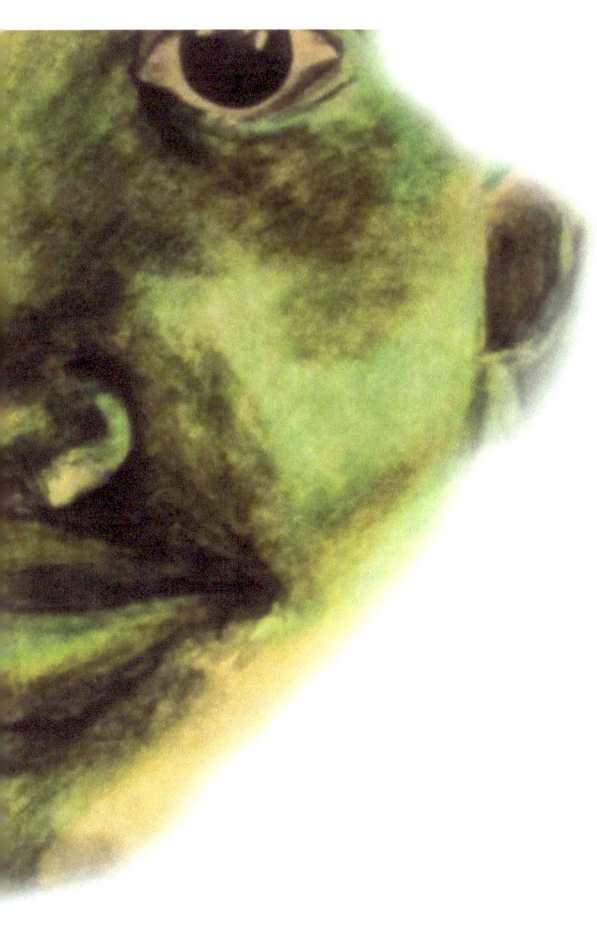

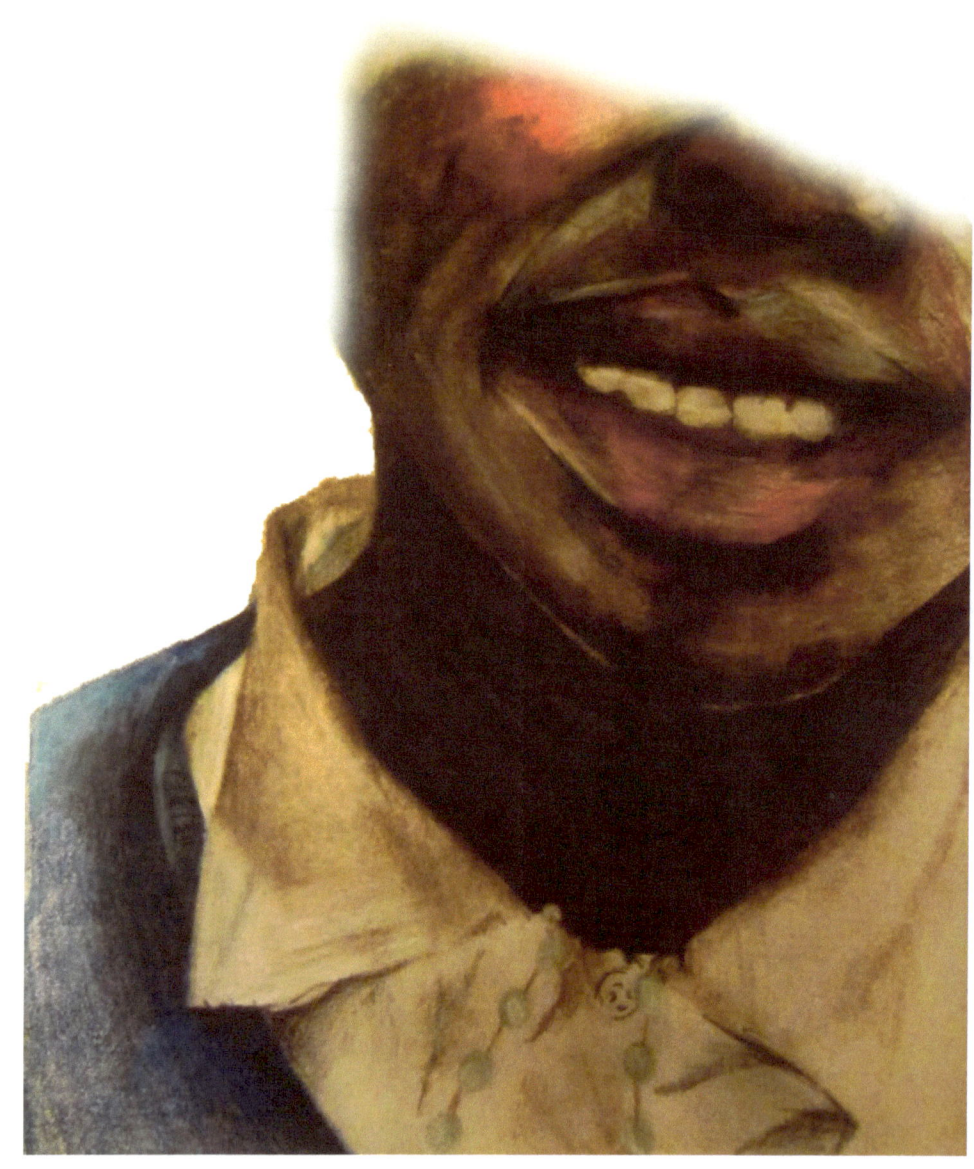

"The Greatest thing you'll ever
learn is just to love
and love
Will be Returned."

-Moulin Rough

Special Thanks To:

My Family. Being the greatest
Supporters &
Friends and Instructors throughout
the years.

Global Alliance Africa:
Thank you for giving me the
opportunity to travel to
Africa and come
back with inspiration and a
touched heart.

Much Love.